The

Redhead
Handbook

The
Redhead
Handbook

Cort Cass

rabbit's
foot
press™

A division of Blue Mountain Arts, Inc.
Boulder, Colorado

Library of Congress Catalog Card Number: 2003010118
ISBN: 1-58786-011-2

Certain trademarks are used under license.

Manufactured in the United States of America.
First Printing: 2003

♲ This book is printed on recycled paper.

This book is printed on fine quality, laid embossed, 80 lb. paper. This paper has been specially produced to be acid free (neutral pH) and contains no groundwood or unbleached pulp. It conforms with all the requirements of the American National Standards Institute, Inc., so as to ensure that this book will last and be enjoyed by future generations.

Library of Congress Cataloging-in-Publication Data

Cass, Cort, 1981-
  The redhead handbook : a fun and comprehensive guide to red hair and more! / by Cort Cass.
      p. cm.
  ISBN 1-58786-011-2 (alk. paper)
  1. Redheads. I. Title.

  GT6735.C37 2003
  391.5—dc21

                                                    2003010118
                                                          CIP

Blue Mountain Arts, Inc.

P.O. Box 4549, Boulder, Colorado 80306

Contents

Introduction

"Why, man, red is the natural color of beauty! What is there that is beautiful or grand in nature or art, that is not tinted with this primordial color?"

— *Mark Twain*

We redheads are a special breed. You can love us or hate us, but you cannot ignore us. We are everywhere these days. Maybe you've seen one of us on television or in an elevator, or maybe you have one of us in your class at school. But chances are, if you are reading this book, you see a beautiful head full of gorgeous red hair every day when you look in the mirror.

No other hair color captures our imagination more. Throughout history, redheads have been objects of intense fascination for artists and writers alike. Today redheads continue to enjoy great success in the spotlight. Whether on film, television, or politics, redheads are constantly in the public eye.

Having been born with fiery red hair, I identify with every other person lucky enough to have been born a redhead. No one else in my immediate family has red hair — my mother and sister are blondes, and my brother and father are brunettes. So my unique coloring was a big deal when I was growing up. Friends, teachers, and strangers wanted to know where my hair came from. Did a distant aunt have it? It must have come from somewhere. Everyone in my family seemed to have a theory about my hair. My older sister was convinced she had the answer: I was a mutant, case closed. Unconvinced, my mother gathered every newspaper and magazine article on red hair she could find. Unfortunately, she did not find many. The science of redheadology is still a very young field.

This book will hopefully satisfy your curiosity about our unique breed. It is for redheads and fans of redheads alike. Have you ever wondered where redheads originally came from? Wondered why you nearly get sunburned from high-wattage light bulbs? Ever speculated about which celebrity redheads were real redheads and which were fake? Well, wonder no more. All of these questions and more will be answered in the coming chapters.

By now, I am sure you are anxious to dive in. That's good. I like that kind of enthusiasm. So, dear reader, put on your rose-colored glasses, and let's begin!

Chapter 1:
Red Hair 101 —
The Science behind the Color

Before we can truly appreciate all there is to know about redheads, we should first appreciate that thing which sets us apart to begin with — our hair! Let's start with the fundamentals. What is it that makes our hair red? Why not purple? Is our hair different for reasons other than color? The following is a crash course on the color and texture of our hair.

Color:

Have you ever stared into the mirror and wondered why your hair radiates that beautiful reddish hue? I sure have. The simple explanation is that you have red hair because someone in your family had red hair and passed it along to you. But we will go over the genetics of red hair in the next chapter (where we will see that the explanation is not so simple). For now, we are just concerned with the chemistry of our hair. If you're like me, the word "chemistry" conjures up bad memories, like the time you had to explain to the fire department that you weren't *trying* to blow up the science lab. Don't worry. You need not have passed high school chemistry to wrap your brain around these concepts.

Melanin:

Put simply, melanin is the reason why you have red hair. Actually, melanin is the reason why anybody has color in his or her hair. Let me explain.

Melanin is a type of pigment, which means it gives color to whatever it is attached to. Human hair is basically made up of protein and moisture. Little bits of melanin lie along these proteins and are spread throughout each hair strand. Got it so far?

There are two types of melanin, one that produces a dark pigment (found in dark-haired individuals) and one that produces a light pigment (found in redheads and blondes). Almost everybody's hair contains a mixture of these two types, which can mix and match in an almost infinite spectrum of potential combinations. Redheads have a large amount of the light-colored melanin, but this amount can vary from redhead to redhead. The amount of this light melanin can vary across your own head and even across individual hair strands (most people's hair is lighter at the tips). What this means is that no two redheads are the same! What kind are you?

Shades of Red:

- *Strawberry Blonde*—probably the sexiest sounding shade of red, strawberry blonde is golden blonde with a slight reddish tint.

- *Golden Red*—think golden retrievers.

- *Copper Red*—looks like the color of copper, hence the moniker "copper-top."

- *Auburn*—the standard color of most redheads. Can be light auburn, medium, or dark.

- *Golden Toasted Auburn*—I just think this sounds cool.

- *Fiery Red*—a.k.a. flaming red, this is a very bright red color.

- *Chestnut Red*—medium-dark auburn with copper highlights.

- *Orange*—what I called my hair when I was growing up. It's unclear whether hair can actually be this color naturally.

The differences in hair color described above might appear subtle. Indeed, the physiological differences underlying these types are even more subtle. Just a slight change in melanin could turn a strawberry blonde into someone with auburn hair. You may or may not fall into any of these categories. Despite being a seasoned red hair specialist, I myself have trouble distinguishing among the shades. To me, my hair is just "red."

As some of you have probably noticed, your hair color may change significantly across your lifetime. This is because the amount of melanin in your hair changes with time. Blonde children, for example, often have brown hair as adults. Many redheads lose their super-special redhead status as they get older. My college roommate had fiery red hair as a child, but now, I'm sorry to say, he is a blonde.

Along the same lines, you may have noticed that redheads don't really gray. There is a scientific explanation for this. Gray hair is caused by the gradual reduction of melanin production over time. The body produces less and less melanin, and the result is a loss of color. The contrast between the hair with more color and the hair with less color causes what appears to be gray hair. But while dark hair and white hair combine to make gray, red hair and white hair do not. Redheads, then, tend to look blonder as they age, not grayer.

It is very difficult to dye naturally red hair. Red hair holds its pigment more tightly than most other colors.

Texture:

Red hair is different from other types of hair in more ways than just its color. Red hair, besides being the most beautiful, is also the thickest. A red hair is more than twice as thick as a blonde hair. But because red hair is so thick, redheads tend to have far fewer strands of hair than other people. Whereas blondes have, on average, 140,000 hairs on their head, redheads have only 90,000. This doesn't necessarily mean that redheaded men are doomed to be bald, however. Because the color of our hair matches the color of our scalp more than in brunettes or darker-haired individuals, we need to lose relatively more hair to give the appearance of being bald. That said, there are quite a few prominent redheads out there who are as bald as cue balls.

Chapter 2:
Survival of the Reddest

In Chapter 1, we learned some background information about the color and structure of our hair. In this chapter, we will go one step further and look at the origins of our hair in evolutionary history. As we will see, not much is known about our ancestors. Some suggest that red hair had its origins in Neanderthals. Others claim that we are all descendants from a great red-haired prince. I myself would rather have a prince as an ancestor than a Neanderthal, but maybe that's just me.

Natural Selection Theory:

In his book *The Origin of Species*, Charles Darwin put forth the idea of "survival of the fittest" to explain evolutionary change. A trait, he wrote, must give some kind of advantage to its host in order for it to be passed on to future generations. If a trait — like long legs, stronger muscles, or better hearing — helps an individual have more babies, then that trait will thrive. A good example of a naturally selected trait is the cheetah's strong legs. During evolutionary history, it paid for cheetahs to have very strong legs. The cheetahs with strong legs were more likely to escape predators and also more likely to be better hunters. The strong-legged cheetahs, being more successful in general, were therefore able to have more babies than their weaker-legged peers, thereby spreading their strong-leg genes to future generations. That's why cheetahs today still have very strong legs.

So is red hair some sort of adaptation? Did it originate in Neanderthals and give our ancestors some kind of advantage that other hair colors did not? The answer is unclear. If anything, red hair might have been a burden to our ncestors. They would have been particularly vulnerable to predators (our friends today still say we are very easy to pick out in a crowd), and their pale skin would have made them more susceptible to sunburn and other environmental dangers.

How can we resolve this? Could red hair have been passed on despite its apparent disadvantages? The answer, since red hair still exists today, is yes. This fact — that apparently disadvantageous traits could survive in a population — bothered Charles Darwin up until the day he died. But what Darwin failed to realize is that a trait could be selected and passed on purely because the opposite sex found it desirable. This is the basic idea of sexual selection theory.

> At the height of the European witch-hunts of the sixteenth and seventeenth centuries, many women were identified as witches and killed merely because they were redheads.

Sexual Selection Theory:

So maybe red hair did not give our ancestors a survival advantage over their peers with other hair colors. But this does not mean that red hair was of no benefit to its bearers. I like to think that red hair might have been a sexually selected trait. What does this mean, exactly?

A sexually selected trait is a trait that comes with no survival advantage, but does give its holder an advantage in the baby-making department. The best example of this is the peacock's tail. In peacocks, unlike humans, the males are the prettier of the two sexes. They develop bright, highly decorative plumage and flaunt it like nobody's business. If anything, these bright fans should be a hindrance to the reproductive success of the peacock. They make their owner more vulnerable to predators and are also very heavy to carry around. But, for whatever reason, female peahens think that these fans are the prettiest things they have ever seen. The males that have the biggest and brightest fans find themselves in huge demand for mating. These males father many babies, while the more boring-looking males do not. In this way, nature has allowed a seemingly troublesome trait to survive.

The same could be true for red hair. Both red hair and peacock's tails have apparent disadvantages and potential costs. Both make their owners more vulnerable to predators. But both of them, for whatever reason, seem to be associated with sexiness and desirability.

There's another question to answer, though. Hair color, like a bright tail, seems like a rather arbitrary signal. Why would we develop a sexual preference for red hair in the first place?

The answer, I think, is that red hair and peacock's tails were used as a sign of other, less obvious, strengths. If a peacock survived to reproductive age despite having a bright and cumbersome plumage, then peahens probably figured he was pretty tough. Peahens used this potential handicap as a cue to identifying reproductively valuable mates. The same reasoning could be applied to red hair. Because redheads were more vulnerable to predators (and also more vulnerable to the sun), those redheads that survived to reproductive age must have been pretty tough. The opposite sex, when deciding whom to mate with, probably recognized this. The redheads that survived and looked healthy, they figured, were probably strong and intelligent. In evolutionary history, then, redheads might have been in huge demand!

Of course, there's always the simple argument that some things just look better. Is there anyone who doesn't agree that peacock fans, like redheads, are gorgeous?

> "While the rest of the human race are descended from monkeys, redheads derive from cats."
>
> — Mark Twain

But Where Did We Come From?

The scientific theories I presented above are just that: theories. No one really knows how redheads evolved. Our evolutionary history is a puzzle. We don't even know where red hair originated. Let's take a look at some possibilities:

The Picts:

Through much of history, the Romans were the only group to mention a faction of redheaded people in their records. These redheads belonged to a group called the Picts, who inhabited what is now Scotland. In the first century A.D., the Romans attempted to subdue the Picts in the Picts' native land. Our redheaded ancestors fought bravely and managed to escape defeat at the hands of the Romans (and they were one of the few groups able to do so).

The Picts were known for being great warriors, but they also appreciated art and literature. Not much else is known about them, though, and they supposedly died out in the ninth century. The idea, though, that the Picts were our first ancestors is a definite possibility. Scotland today has the largest proportion of redheads in the world, with a full thirteen percent of the population sporting red hair.

The Red-Haired Prince:

Legend has it that the first redhead was a Prince Idon of Mu. During a visit to an oracle, Prince Idon learned that his land was destined to be destroyed by a natural catastrophe. Alarmed, Prince Idon gathered his followers and set sail for Atlantis. After a long and dangerous trip, his fleet finally arrived at sunset. Prince Idon was extremely moved by the gorgeous red hues that radiated across the sky from the setting sun. He marveled at the striking leaves that seemed to dance in the wind. He was so struck that he wished aloud that the image be saved for generations to come. His wish was granted. His hair turned a beautiful shade of red that matched the sun and sky. His face was colored with a sprinkling of freckles that matched the color of the leaves. All of his descendants inherited this same look, forever reminding people of that first sunset in Atlantis. The implications of this story are tremendous. Since we are all descendants from Prince Idon, we are all royalty!

That's Great! But Why Do I Have Red Hair?

That's an easy enough question. You have red hair because you have the gene for red hair.

Actually, it's not quite that simple.

Red hair is a recessive trait. From what I remember from high school biology, this means that you must inherit one red hair gene from each parent in order to be a copper-top. Only those individuals that do so will win the genetic hair lottery. Brown and other hair colors are dominant over red. So if you inherit the gene for brown hair from one parent and the gene for red hair from the other, you will unfortunately be a brunette. But don't worry, there is hope for your offspring. Because you carry the gene for red hair (but don't show it), it is possible for your child to have red hair if your partner also carries the gene. I myself was born to a brunette and a blonde. What, might you ask, happens when both the mother and father are redheads? You guessed it: a copper-top every time.

> Apparently recessive traits come in pairs. Redheads are more likely than other people to be left-handed.

The fact that people can have the gene for red hair without actually having a head full of red hair is cool for two reasons. First, these people may be able to grow red beards despite being brown on top. I have several brunette friends who found out, once puberty hit, that their facial hair was redder than mine! Non-redheaded women who carry the redhead gene can also express it in weird ways, though sometimes they need a little push from nature. My mother, who is a sandy blonde, mysteriously began to grow red hairs near the part in her hair when she was pregnant with me. Since she was sharing much-needed nourishment, I must have thought it only fair that I share my red hair in return. I took them back, though, as soon as I was born.

Second, this means that redheads have a built-in safety net should anyone try to eliminate us completely. Even if every redhead on Earth were destroyed (out of jealousy or bizarre anti-redhead prejudice), our red hair would live on through non-redheads who carry our gene. So let's recap. Not only are redheads princes and princesses, but we are also indestructible!

Chapter 3:
Historical Redheads

At the end of Chapter 2, we learned that redheads are indestructible. So what have we done with our invincibility? The answer is, a lot! A brief glimpse through our history books reveals a surprising number of copper-tops. Redheads, it seems, are natural leaders. Whether in art, literature, or politics, redheads have dominated their fields. Let's take a closer look at some of the more noteworthy redheads in history.

Redheads in Ancient History:

Adam – First Man. There is speculation that Adam, of Garden of Eden fame, was a redhead. The Bible relates that Adam was formed of "red earth." In fact, the Hebrew word for red is "Adom." Does this mean that all humans were meant to be redheads?

Judas Iscariot – Informer. It is rumored that Judas was a fiery redhead. Perhaps this explains why we have gained the reputation for being untrustworthy.

Nero – Roman Emperor. The last in line of the great Julio-Claudian dynasty, Nero was descended from Julius Caesar and Caesar Augustus. Though he was somewhat of an outcast, this had more to do with his out-of-control insanity than with his red hair.

Explorers:

Eric the Red – Norwegian Navigator. In the tenth century, Eric the Red founded the first European settlement on Greenland. Leif Ericsson, his red-haired son and a famous explorer in his own right, may well have been the first redhead to set foot in North America.

Christopher Columbus – Explorer. "In 1492, Columbus sailed the ocean blue" and opened the way for European exploration and colonization of the Americas. His suggestion of "The Copper-Top Express" for the name of one of the boats was rejected in favor of "Nina." Or was it "Pinta?"

Royalty and Government:

William the Conqueror – King of England. The illegitimate son of the Duke of Normandy, William the Conqueror invaded and conquered England in the eleventh century. His boldness is pretty typical of a redhead.

King Henry VIII – King of England. Henry VIII ruled England for thirty-eight years in the beginning of the sixteenth century. The significance of his reign is overshadowed by the scandalous circumstances surrounding his six marriages (only three were to fellow redheads).

Queen Elizabeth I – Queen of England, Daughter of Henry VIII. Known as the "Virgin Queen" because she never married, Elizabeth I ruled England for forty-four years in the late sixteenth century. Though she was born with red hair, an experimental hair-washing session with lye made her hair fall out. Her red wig made flame-colored tresses fashionable in England at the time.

Napoleon Bonaparte – French Emperor. One of the greatest military generals of all time, Napoleon's conquests threatened the stability of the world. Though rumored to be incredibly short, Napoleon was actually 5'7", the average height of a Frenchman of his day.

Oliver Cromwell – British Monarch. Known as something of an enigma, Cromwell was a devout Puritan who ruled England as "Lord Protector" in the middle of the seventeenth century. As commander-in-chief of the army, he was able to seize control of the government and helped make England a feared and respected world power.

Academia, Art, and Literature:

Galileo Galilei – Italian Physicist and Astronomer. Galileo's invention of the microscope and his work in mechanics proved very influential, but Galileo is best remembered for his work in astronomy. He discovered the satellites of Jupiter and defended Copernican astronomy, a stance that eventually resulted in his exile.

Vincent Van Gogh – Dutch Painter. Van Gogh's copper red hair can be seen in any one of his many self-portraits. Working in the late nineteenth century, Van Gogh constantly battled poverty, alcoholism, and his own inner demons. Though now regarded as one of the greatest artists in history, he sold only one painting during his lifetime.

Antonio Vivaldi – Italian Composer. Best known for his piece "The Four Seasons," Vivaldi was actually trained for the priesthood before finding his calling in music. Because of this (and his fiery red hair), he was known as "The Red Priest."

William Blake – Romantic Poet, Artist. Blake, a Brit born in the middle of the eighteenth century, was one of the earliest and greatest figures of Romanticism. He was very fond of redheads. He wrote: "The ruddy limbs and flaming hair… plant fruits of life and beauty there."

William Shakespeare – British Playwright. The most famous playwright of all time, Shakespeare was supposedly born a redhead. Though his hair eventually turned brown, we will gladly accept him as part of our legacy.

Lord Byron – Nineteenth-Century British Poet. Born George Gordon, Lord Byron was a temperamental figure whose disposition matched his fiery locks. His licentious verse and debauched lifestyle made him somewhat of a villain in his homeland.

Emily Dickinson – American Lyrical Poet. Working in the nineteenth century at the time of the Civil War, Dickinson penned more than 1800 poems. Dickinson wasn't your typical outgoing redhead. A homebody by nature, she secluded herself in her Amherst, Massachusetts, home.

Other Celebrities:

Lizzie Borden – Accused Murderess. Lizzie Borden captured the attention of the national media during her trial for the murder of her parents in 1892. Although she was acquitted, many people were convinced this hot-tempered redhead was guilty.

General Custer – Military General. Born George Armstrong Custer, General Custer invoked the bold redhead spirit and led his troops to numerous victories during the end of the Civil War. He is perhaps best known, though, for his "last stand" against the Sioux and Cheyenne at the Battle of Little Bighorn.

Jesse James – Outlaw. A hero to some, a villain to most, Jesse James is the most famous redhead criminal. His daring bank robberies have made him a legend.

Florence Nightingale – Nurse Extraordinaire. Nightingale revolutionized the British health-care system in the nineteenth century, a time when most Victorian women did not attend university or pursue professional careers. There's that classic redhead boldness and tenacity at work again!

> Redheads have been the objects of intense fascination for many artists. In Renaissance paintings, red-haired subjects are more common than brunette, blonde, or black-haired subjects.

United States Presidents:

At last count, redheads made up approximately four percent of the population here in the United States. Can you believe, then, that almost twenty percent of United States presidents have been redheads? A startling fact indeed.

And while many of them were either bald or had white hair by the time they reached office, they still grew up red. So what makes redheads so adept at ruling the free world? Maybe it's our natural charisma. Or perhaps it's our incredible intellect. Or maybe it's that intangible something that draws people to redheads. In any case, here is a list of the copper-topped presidents who have overseen the rule of our great country:

George Washington – First President of the United States
Thomas Jefferson – Third President of the United States
Martin Van Buren – Eighth President of the United States
Andrew Jackson – Seventeenth President of the United States
Ulysses S. Grant – Eighteenth President of the United States
Calvin Coolidge – Thirtieth President of the United States
Dwight Eisenhower – Thirty-fourth President of the United States

Chapter 4:

Recent Remarkable Redheads

Redheads have truly made their mark. The previous chapter, a list of some of the most famous redheads of all time, reads like a "Who's Who in World History." It's exciting to think that redheads have changed the fate of the world with their accomplishments. But what about redheads in the twentieth century? Have they been as influential as other redheads in history? The answer is yes, and perhaps even more so. These days it seems like anybody who is anybody is a redhead.

All right, maybe that's not quite true. But redheads do seem to be everywhere. I could probably fill this whole book with the names of redheads who have made their mark during the past one hundred years. But that seems a bit excessive (and a little too boastful). Instead, here is a list of some of the most visible redheads who have helped shape this past century.

Real or Fake?

Thanks to the explosion of the hair coloring market, there are countless fake redheads out there today. Think you've got what it takes to tell a real redhead from a fake one? Try these:

1. Mark McGwire
2. Tori Amos
3. Shirley Manson, lead singer of Garbage
4. Debra Messing, co-star of *Will & Grace*
5. Lucille Ball
6. Julia Roberts
7. Nicole Kidman
8. Chuck Norris
9. Sarah McLachlan
10. Ronald McDonald

Answers: 1) real, 2) fake, 3) real, 4) fake, 5) fake, 6) fake, 7) real, 8) real, 9) fake, 10) real.

Politics and Royalty:

Winston Churchill – That's Sir Winston Churchill to you. As Prime Minister of England during World War II, this courageous redhead led the British people from the brink of defeat.

Vladimir Lenin – Famous for his Marxist speeches and political instinct, this Soviet leader founded Bolshevism and helped secure the revolutionary party as a force in politics. Though most redheads are not communists, our "red history" was truly red in Lenin's case.

Prince Henry – Third in line to the throne, Harry is a favorite of British tabloids. A redheaded king? England should be so lucky.

Sarah Ferguson – a.k.a. Fergie. One of the most visible redheads today, the Duchess of York is another favorite of British tabloids. The scandals, though, overshadow her success in charity work and as a children's book author.

Writers:

Sylvia Plath – An extremely gifted and accomplished poet, Plath found solace from her depression in writing. Unfortunately, she killed herself while she was still in her prime.

James Joyce – A true redheaded Irishman, Joyce is considered by some to be the most significant writer of the twentieth century. His mastery of the English language can be best seen in *Ulysses*.

Ezra Pound – Pound was a controversial American poet — a traitor to some, an idol to others. Pound encouraged fellow redhead James Joyce to pursue writing as a career.

D. H. Lawrence – British author D. H. Lawrence was one of the most influential fiction writers of the twentieth century. His lyrical writing style often called for a return to nature.

Mark Twain – As many of his quotes show, Samuel L. Clemens (a.k.a. Mark Twain) loved red hair. Indeed, this *Huckleberry Finn* author was a carrot-top himself.

J. K. Rowling – The *Harry Potter* series has made the redheaded Rowling the wealthiest female wage earner in Great Britain. But why didn't she make Harry a redhead? Oh well.

George Bernard Shaw – His *Pygmalion* later became *My Fair Lady.* When told by a model that they could have remarkable children, Shaw quipped: "Ah, yes… But what if they had my looks and your brain?"

Tom Wolfe – Always seen publicly in his impeccable white suits, Wolfe is an American literary icon. His best-known work, *The Electric Kool-Aid Acid Test*, is a non-fiction account of the hippie world.

Television and Movies:

Conan O'Brien – The king of late night, the famously red-haired O'Brien honed his comedic skills as president of the *Harvard Lampoon*.

Redhead Stars

Katherine Hepburn – Hepburn's staying power in Hollywood is unparalleled. She won four academy awards, first for *Morning Glory* (1932) and 50 years later for *On Golden Pond* (1982).

Eric Stoltz – One of the great redhead leading men on the silver screen today, Stoltz has garnered critical praise for his performances in movies like *The Mask*, *Little Women*, and *Pulp Fiction*.

David Caruso – Best known as Detective John Kelly on *N.Y.P.D. Blue*, Caruso left the show unexpectedly after one season. Perhaps he was upset that he was the only redhead in the cast.

Susan Hayward – One of the most talented redhead actresses of all time, Hayward enjoyed a career that spanned several decades. Hayward was nominated for four Academy Awards before finally winning for *I Want to Live*.

Arthur Godfrey – Nicknamed "Old Redhead," Godfrey was successful as both a radio and a television personality.

Woody Allen – Woody Allen has enjoyed incredible success as a writer, director, and actor. His self-deprecating humor has helped make him one of the biggest draws in Hollywood.

Ron Howard – Ron Howard has been a television and movie star ever since he first appeared on fellow redhead Red Skelton's show when he was just a tot. Though he is perhaps most famous for his roles as Richie Cunningham in *Happy Days* and Opie in *The Andy Griffith Show*, he is also an accomplished director, having recently won an Academy Award for *A Beautiful Mind*.

Nicole Kidman – Stunningly beautiful, Kidman is an accomplished actress whose talent is just as remarkable as her beauty.

Shirley Temple Black – The curly-haired and dimpled Shirley Temple remains one of the most successful childhood actors of all time. She followed her acting career by becoming active in the Republican Party, serving under Ford, Nixon, and Bush.

Red Skelton – One of the most popular comedians of the twentieth century, Red Skelton won over audiences with both a radio and a television show. *The Red Skelton Show* ran on CBS for over twenty years.

Julianne Moore – Called the "thinking man's sex symbol," Moore is a talented actress whose credits include *Boogie Nights*, *Hannibal*, and *Magnolia*.

Marilyn Monroe – The ultimate sex symbol of the twentieth century, Monroe was supposedly born a copper-top. Hard to believe, I know.

Robert Redford – The Sundance Kid's boyish good looks have helped make him one of the biggest stars in Hollywood. A talented actor and director, Redford founded the Sundance Institute to help young filmmakers.

Ted Koppel – Although his red hair has faded, Koppel was born a redhead in Lancashire, England. His *Nightline* has helped make him one of the world's most popular broadcast journalists.

Music:

Mick Hucknall – Mick Hucknall is the lead singer of a fantastic group called Simply Red. How appropriate!

Geri Halliwell – Geri was everyone's favorite Spice Girl (well, at least she was my favorite). Though she left the group to pursue a solo career, she will always remain Ginger Spice to me.

Bonnie Raitt – With her powerful bluesy voice, this flame-haired country superstar is one of the few musicians to make a successful comeback.

Van Morrison – Born George Ivan Morrison in Northern Ireland, Van Morrison was one of the most influential singer/songwriters of the 60s and 70s. His *Moondance* deserves a spot in every record collection.

Willie Nelson – Nelson is widely credited for inventing the "outlaw" style of country music. He is a gentle soul at heart, though; he organizes Farm Aid concerts to raise money for farmers. *Red Headed Stranger* is one of his most famous albums.

Reba McEntire – Reba is perhaps the most famous and successful country and western singer today. Her career has spanned several decades, two Grammy Awards, and countless sold-out shows.

Axl Rose – This front man of Guns N' Roses certainly has the fiery temper to match his fiery locks. There's no reason to be angry, though; Guns N' Roses has sold millions and millions of records.

Fictitious Characters:

Nancy Drew – Though she doesn't look a day over sixteen, Nancy Drew has been solving mysteries for over seven decades. A great role model for girls everywhere, this redhead can really do it all.

Ronald McDonald – Keep up that shining smile, Ronald. Not only were you blessed with red hair, but you are also the most famous and richest clown out there.

Ariel – The world's most famous mermaid, Ariel is a rare find. Did you know that only one percent of mermaids are redheads?

Anne of Green Gables – Set in 1890s Canada, the story of this irrepressible redheaded orphan has inspired countless books, movies, and television programs.

Alfred E. Neuman – One of the world's most recognizable mascots, this prankster was *Mad Magazine*'s cover model and spokesperson for several decades.

Groundskeeper Willie – One of The *Simpsons'* most lovable characters, Willie has paraded his Scottish roots and chiseled body around Springfield ever since the first season.

Elmo – Elmo consistently ranks as the most popular Muppet on *Sesame Street*. What's not to like about him? He enjoys tap dancing, rollerblading, and miniature golf.

Howdy Doody – The freckle-faced puppet entertained children through thirteen seasons and 2,343 episodes. Though the show was canceled over forty years ago, redheaded boys are constantly reminded of their striking resemblance to Howdy. Enough already!

Little Orphan Annie – Despite being born in 1924, Little Orphan Annie has the spunkiness of girls one-tenth her age! Her crazy adventures can still be seen in comic strips around the country.

Peppermint Patty – Though she is a slacker in school, Patty is an all-star on the baseball field. What she doesn't want you to know is that she is secretly in love with Charlie Brown.

Archie Andrews – The star of *Archie Comics*, Archie Andrews is your all-American teenager. Whether chasing after Veronica, hanging out at Pop's, or goofing off at school, Archie just wants to have fun. Everybody loves Archie!

Pippi Longstocking – Pippi is a nine-year-old redheaded girl who happens to have a pot of gold and superhuman strength! With no patience for school, Pippi lives out all of our dreams by spending her days scrubbing the floor with her feet and hanging out with her pet monkey.

Chuckie of *The Rugrats* – He comes across as a scaredy-cat, but by the time he reaches the finish line he always gathers strength and courage and even becomes a heroic figure. Go, Chuckie!

Chapter 5:
Sunlight is the Enemy and Other Redhead Challenges

A redhead's life isn't all fun and games. We may be extremely successful, but nature has played a cruel trick or two on us. Perhaps she did this to even the score for all our natural gifts?

The sun and I have always had a love/hate relationship. To me, there is nothing more peaceful than soaking up the sun under a perfectly blue sky. Unfortunately, there is nothing more painful than the second-degree sunburn that invariably follows. I seem to get sunburned in places that most people do not (like my scalp and the tops of my hands and feet). On a recent road trip, I managed to get a sunburn through my car windshield, which should be physically impossible. Sometimes it seems like I can get burned from a light bulb.

When I was younger, my family had to plan vacations around my propensity to burn. Tropical locations were out of the question — the sun would be too brutal. Ski trips also proved to be problematic. At high altitudes, the sun gave my delicate, pasty skin a beating. I did manage to convince my parents to take me to Disneyland when I was five years old. And while I was so excited on the first day that I forgot to wear underpants, I did remember to wear my SPF 45 sunscreen.

Being a redhead means being careful in the sun. Like gremlins, sun rays are crueler than they appear. Here is everything a redhead needs to know about our common enemy, sunlight.

UV Rays:

Sunlight is made up of three kinds of ultraviolet rays: UVA, UVB, and UVC rays. UVA and UVB rays are the most harmful. UVA rays are known as "aging rays." They were once thought to be harmless, but now they are believed to be the cause of wrinkles and sunspots. UVB rays are "burning rays." These rays seem to prey on redheads. They almost immediately cause sunburn, and prolonged exposure to them may cause skin cancer later in life.

UVB rays are one hundred times more intense than their UVA counterparts. Luckily, UVC rays are not considered a threat because they are blocked by the ozone layer.

Sunburns:

Most redheads are familiar with the cycle that sunburns follow. After a relaxing and enjoyable day in the sun, we come home to discover that our arms (and chest, and back, and toes) are red. These burns soon become painful. That night we sleep on our side to ease the searing pain. The pain and redness goes away in a few days and then we begin to peel. The next week we ignore our previous mistake and repeat the cycle.

Though all skin types are susceptible to sunburns, redheads seem most vulnerable. Why does the sun hate us so? Interestingly, the answer to this question is the same answer I gave in Chapter 1 to the "Why is our hair red?" question. Here again, the wonder agent responsible is melanin. Not only does melanin give our hair color, but it also determines our skin color. Dark-skinned individuals simply have more melanin than us fair-skinned people. When our dark-skinned friends go out in the sun, they produce more melanin and look tanner. But redheads (and other people with light skin) do not produce melanin as easily. Therefore, we burn.

If it's any comfort, some people have it worse than we do. Albinos lack the ability to produce melanin at all and thus are even more susceptible to sunburns. So next time you're walking down the street with your albino friend, be considerate. Let him share your sun umbrella.

Freckles:

I love my freckles. I may not always have liked them, but they have definitely grown on me. But where did they come from? After a little legwork, I found two competing theories. The first is scientific. Freckles are small patches of melanin that accumulate in the skin. Sometimes freckles are present at birth. Other freckles may appear as a response to the sun.

The other theory is that freckles are "angel kisses." Legend has it that everyone has an angel who watches over him. If your angel thinks that you have been good, she will come down in the middle of the night and kiss you! Looking around, it seems like angels disproportionately favor redheads. As well they should!

Whichever explanation you like better, be proud of your freckles. I personally think freckles are pretty, and many people would agree with me. If you are lucky enough to have them, show them off!

> Harvard dermatologist Madhu Pathak calls redheads "three-time losers" because their skin is more susceptible to sunburn, skin cancer, and wrinkling with age.

Premature Aging:

Not all of the sun's effects can be seen immediately. With chronic exposure, sunlight can eventually ruin that pretty mug of yours. UVA rays in sunlight can cause premature aging even if your skin does not burn easily. These rays can give your skin a thick, leathery look and feel as you get older. People who spend a lot of time in the sun tend to wrinkle more quickly than those who do not. These people may also get unsightly sunspots (solar keratoses) from the sun. Some people think that an aging, weathered look is an unavoidable part of growing older. It's not. I think redheads tend to age really well. Stay out of the sun, and let's keep it that way!

Skin Cancer:

Skin cancer is a far more serious concern of redheads. Skin cancer is the most common cancer in the United States. The statistics are staggering. Over 1.3 million new cases of skin cancer are diagnosed in the United States each year. It is one of only two types of cancer in the United States that continue to increase rather than decrease. One in six Americans will develop skin cancer in their lifetime. Unfortunately, this number is even higher for redheads.

There are essentially two types of skin cancer: melanoma and non-melanoma cancer. Melanoma is much rarer, but it accounts for most skin cancer-related deaths. Melanoma is found across all age groups and can occur anywhere on the body. Because it comes from too much sun exposure, women most often get it on their legs and men usually get it on their backs. Beware of any new moles on your body or any old moles that appear to be growing in size, are uneven in color, or have an irregular shape. If you find an unusual mole, get it checked by a doctor.

Although any person, regardless of age, sex, or race, can get skin cancer, there are certain people who are at more risk than others. Some of the risk factors include

- Blonde/red hair
- Blue/green eyes
- Being a woman (compared to men, women are twice as likely to develop malignant melanoma)
- Fair skin with lots of freckles
- Spending a lot of time outdoors
- Sunbathing, especially in the tropics
- Indoor workers with pale skin, who sit out in strong sunlight during the summer
- Severe sunburns in the past
- Lots of moles
- Family history of skin cancer
- Growing up in the South or Midwest

Chances are, if you are a redhead, many of these risk factors apply to you. It is unclear why redheads are at such a high risk of developing skin cancer. Scientific research has largely been unhelpful, but there are findings that suggest that the reason is genetic. Melanoma has been linked to variations in a certain gene that most redheads share. If you carry this gene, you are much more likely to get melanoma in your lifetime. And if you have a family history of skin cancer, you probably have this gene.

Given the enormous strides that have been made in genetic research, it may soon be possible to substantially cut the number of melanoma cases in this country. Until then, redheads should be careful to protect themselves from the sun.

Sun Protection:

As we have seen, redheads and sunlight do not mix well. Redheads should take great care to protect themselves. Here are some suggestions:

- Stay in the shade! The simplest and most effective way to protect yourself from the sun is to limit the time you spend absorbing it. Try to avoid being outdoors in the sun for too long. And if you are going to the beach, bring a beach umbrella.
- Use sunscreen!
- Buy sunscreen that has at least a 30 SPF. SPF stands for "sun protection factor." An SPF of 30 allows you to stay in the sun thirty times longer than you could without it. So if you normally start to burn after five minutes in the sun (like most redheads), an SPF of 30 will allow you to spend 30 x 5 = 150 minutes in the sun. Ideally, redheads should use the sunscreen that has the highest possible SPF.
- Use a waterproof sunscreen if you are going to the pool or beach.
- Avoid the sun between 10 a.m. and 3 p.m. Its rays are strongest during this time.
- Be careful in tropical climates or at high altitudes. The sun is deceptively strong.
- Don't be fooled by cloudy skies! Up to eighty percent of UV rays can pass through clouds.
- Don't use sunlamps or tanning beds! They emit the highest levels of UV radiation.
- Be careful in the pool and at the beach. Both sand and water tend to reflect light.
- Watch out if you are on any medications. Some medications make you more vulnerable to the sun.
- Wear sunglasses! Overexposure to UV rays can lead to cataracts and macular degeneration. Both of these can cause blindness later in life.
- If you must have a golden tanned look, consider using a self-tanner. The acceptance of self-tanners has grown considerably as people have become more wary of the effects of a natural tan. Remember, though, that self-tanners provide no protection against the sun. Don't forget to wear sunscreen!

Redheads everywhere should practice smart sun protection. It can be difficult, though, to keep sunscreen handy at all times. Don't be afraid to be creative in your battle against the sun. One of my father's friends, a redhead from Pittsburgh, spent a lot of time outdoors when she was growing up. To protect her from the sun, her father used to spread mud all over her cheeks, nose, and shoulders when she went outside. This probably wasn't the most attractive thing, but it served its purpose well.

A good imagination can be just as effective as sunscreen at protecting against the sun's harmful UV rays. As long as you keep an open mind, you should be fine. Forgot to bring sunscreen to the beach again? Don't sweat it. Have your friend turn you into a human sandcastle.

Chapter 6:
The Three Biggest Myths about Redheads

Because we redheads are so rare, people tend to misunderstand us. It's surprising how ignorant people can be sometimes. These misconceptions can often be insulting, but some are so ridiculous that they are laughable. Here I present the top three misconceptions about redheads.

The Big Three:

1) We are all related.

For some strange reason, people think that all redheads are related. Never mind the fact that redheads have existed for thousands of years and reside in all parts of the world. If two redheads are seen together, then they must automatically be related. Surprisingly, this will happen even if one of the redheads is significantly taller and has completely different facial features. I have no living redheaded relatives. If a redhead looks like me, it is pure coincidence. So don't ask if we are related!

Growing up, there were always a handful of other redheads at my school. Classmates and teachers alike often confused me with other redheaded students. This phenomenon seemed to follow me everywhere.

> Scotland boasts the highest number of redheads per capita, with thirteen percent of the population seeing red when they look in the mirror. Ireland follows second with ten percent. The United States falls in at a paltry four percent.

At summer camp, my fellow campers sometimes confused me with Patrick, the one kid at camp whom everyone hated. If they didn't think I was Patrick, they assumed I was Patrick's brother. It didn't help that Patrick had poofy orange hair and made the girls run away when he approached. Pretty soon the girls were running away from me as well. "I'm not Patrick!" I would scream. They didn't listen.

2) We are all Irish.

Let me begin by saying that I have nothing against the Irish. I think they are great. I really do. I, however, am not one of them. Though I can do a great Irish accent and can dance a mean jig, my roots lie elsewhere.

At parties, people will often feed me drinks under the assumption that I can drink like my supposed Irish brethren. Little do they know that I have the tolerance of a fourteen-year-old girl. At some of these same parties, I am also asked whether I plan on visiting my homeland. I could see asking a Kelly or O'Brien this question, but a Cass? Last time I checked, Cass was German. Perhaps I should just go along with it. That would make it easier for everyone. Besides, I've always wanted to wear green on St. Patrick's Day.

3) We are all crazy, excitable, hot-tempered...

Much has been made about the nature of redhead personalities. People mistakenly assume that we have fiery tempers to match our fiery hair. This is, like most stereotypes, simply untrue. We are no crazier than the average blonde or brunette. I myself am a relatively calm, laid-back guy. Let's hang out sometime. I'll show you.

Most of my redheaded friends are equally laid-back. We don't get riled up very easily. Redheads learn at a pretty young age to roll with the punches. It's just not worth it to get upset every time a comment is made about our hair. Besides, I was always smaller than everyone else. A quick wit was just as effective as a quick fist.

More often than not it seems like other people, not redheads themselves, are the crazy ones. For some reason, people tend to get excited when they see a redhead. Sometimes they do a double take. Often they stare. Sometimes they seem more confrontational. Why is this? Does the color red incite some primordial passion in them?

Possibly so. Red is the color of blood. During our evolution, the sight of blood signaled that food was available. Our ancestors had to fight each other for access to this food. Does this mean that people want to fight over us because they are looking for dinner? Maybe. Watch out.

I must admit, though, that I know a few redheads who fit the stereotype exactly. They are crazy and excitable. They say outrageous things and love to be the center of attention. But I doubt that they were born that way. If anything, they are the result of a self-fulfilling prophecy. The way we treat people has a lot to do with the way they treat us. If people expect us to be hot-tempered and excitable, then they may change their behavior accordingly. Consciously or unconsciously, we may begin to alter our behavior to fit others' expectations. In this way, redheads may develop personalities to match the stereotypes. I can assure you, though, that by nature we are a very gentle breed!

Chapter 7:
Nicknames —
Please Don't Call Me "Red"

My name is Cort. It really isn't that hard to remember. Think tennis court, basketball court, court of law, quart of milk. If you don't remember my name, you can always call me "Red." Everyone else does. Such is the life of a redhead. For some reason, people we have never met act like they know us. "Hey, Red!" they'll call out. This really works only with us. If I respond with "Hey, Blonde!" or "Hey, Brown!", they will usually look at me as if I'm crazy. Can't take a taste of your own medicine, eh?

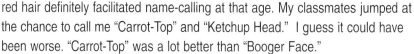

For many people, it seems like our red hair is our defining characteristic. I guess it's only natural that we are given redheaded nicknames. The nicknames, for me at least, began around the time of kindergarten. Having red hair definitely facilitated name-calling at that age. My classmates jumped at the chance to call me "Carrot-Top" and "Ketchup Head." I guess it could have been worse. "Carrot-Top" was a lot better than "Booger Face."

Over the years, I have been "red"-iculed many times because of my hair. I hated it when I was younger, but I have slowly gotten used to the attention. And while I no longer get "Ketchup Head," I'm still called "Red" and "Rusty" on occasion.

Here is a list of my top five hated nicknames:
1) Carrot-Top — This hardly makes sense. Carrot tops are green!
2) Raggedy Ann — I would have been completely OK with "Raggedy Andy," though.

3) Big Red — I am short. That is why this is funny.
4) Ronald McDonald's Illegitimate Child
5) Howdy Doody

There are countless other nicknames for redheads out there. If you are a redhead, then you probably have heard many of these. If these bring back bad memories of teasing, then I'm sorry. Get over it already!

Red

Flame

Little Red

Strawberry Shortcake

Reddy

Woody Woodpecker

Roja

Scarlet

Satan's Love Child

Pippi Longstocking

Irish

Ketchup Head

Bloody

Carrot Soup

Freckle Face

Chocolate Chip Face

Duracell

Carrot the Red

Casper

Bloody Locks

Ginger

Flamey

Little Orphan Annie

Howdy Doody

Red on the Head

Penny

Peliroja

Red Hot Chili Pepper

Tomato Head

Chuckie

Copper-Top

Redheaded Goddess

Rusty

Freckles

Freckle Nation

Viking Steve

Copper Head

Bozo the Clown

Powder

Bluey

Chapter 8:
Bottle Reds — a.k.a. Wannabes, Posers, Cheap Imitations

Redheads are fantastic. So fantastic, in fact, that there are countless people out there who go to great lengths to join our ranks. Hair salons go through an incredible amount of red hair dye each year. In fact, red is the most requested color at beauty salons. Since seventy-five percent of American women admit to coloring their hair, this means there are a lot of fake redheads.

Author Rant:

There are more fake redheads than one might imagine. Unfortunately, these wannabes are stealing our thunder. There are actually more fakers out there than true redheads. This is certainly a shame. What fun is it being a redhead if you aren't unique?

I have the same problem with colored contact lenses. In my experience, most redheads have beautiful eyes. Whether blue, green, or hazel (or, like me, some ever-changing combination thereof), our eyes stand out. It's one of the great things about being a redhead. But it becomes less special when a random person can walk into a store and buy any set of eyes he or she desires.

But maybe I'm just greedy. I can see the other side of the debate as well. Perhaps dyed red hair is a compliment to natural redheads. I should be excited that other people want to adopt our hair color. Imitation is the best form of flattery, after all.

It does bother me, though, that the same people who teased us as children are now paying to become redheads themselves! It seems that, once we pass a certain age, it suddenly becomes very cool to have red hair. This shouldn't happen. Red hair is timeless. It should not be a fad or a trend. Red hair is always in style!

A redhead knows a fake redhead when he or she sees one. We are not easily fooled. Having lived with red hair our entire lives, we can easily discriminate between the lucky ones and the fakers. Some wannabes, though, will never admit that their hair color comes from a bottle. That's fine. But there are so many fakers out there that we real redheads are sometimes questioned about our own tresses. "Is it real?" random people will ask. Of course it is!

The fact of the matter is that real redheads are born, not made. As much as others might try to emulate us, they will never be true redheads.

Some Famous Bottle Reds:

Cleopatra – This legendary beauty and Egyptian queen used henna to add red highlights to her hair. This fact probably didn't help her cause. The Romans attributed typical redhead stereotypes to her — calling her domineering, deceitful, and evil.

Gillian Anderson – A redhead sex symbol, Gillian Anderson has won over countless fans as the rational skeptic Scully on *The X-Files*. Does her dyed red hair help her solve supernatural and paranormal problems? Probably.

> Red hair dye fades faster than other hair dyes. Some beauty salons encourage their clients to go red just because it's more expensive to maintain.

Rita Hayworth – Rita's decision to become a redhead was one of the best career decisions she made. Soon after she went red, she became a huge Hollywood star and famous World War II pinup.

Tori Amos – One of the coolest singer/songwriters of our time, this famously redheaded musician gets her color straight from a bottle.

Lucille Ball – America's most beloved redhead, Lucille Ball remains one of the funniest female actresses of all time. She supposedly went through gallons and gallons of henna during her *I Love Lucy* reign.

Claire Danes – Her *So-Called Life* was a critically acclaimed show on ABC until it was mysteriously canceled after only nineteen episodes. Did a top exec discover that her hair was fake?

Lauren Holly – This sexy actress is best known for her smart, elegant role opposite Jim Carrey in *Dumb and Dumber*. What better way to contrast Carrey's dim-witted character than with an intelligent redheaded heroine?

Susan Sarandon – This bottle red has starred in countless movies over the years (*Thelma & Louise, The Rocky Horror Picture Show*, etc.) and finally won an Oscar for *Dead Man Walking*.

Sissy Spacek – Spacek ranks as one of the most accomplished actresses of all time. Her fiery tresses (though fake) have appeared in more than forty feature and television films. She has been nominated for seven "Best Actress" Academy Awards and won for *Coal Miner's Daughter*.

Bette Midler – First discovered by Barry Manilow, this sometimes fake redhead has recorded a number of hit records while also becoming a crossover star in such films as *The Rose* and *Down and Out in Beverly Hills*.

Kate Winslet – After dyeing her hair for the part, Winslet became a certified A-list celebrity with her breakout performance as the red Rose in *Titanic*.

Elton John – One of the biggest pop stars of the past three decades, Elton charted a Top 40 single every year from 1970 to 1996. He was born as a brunette named Reginald Dwight.

Julia Roberts – The object of many a man's fantasy, Julia Roberts particularly wowed audiences as the redheaded Vivian Ward in *Pretty Woman*. But isn't every redheaded lady a "pretty woman"?

Henna — Nature's Quick Fix:

There are really only two ways to have red hair. One way, obviously, is to be born with it. The other is to fake it. And while I do not condone this practice, I will not stop anyone who has his or her mind set on becoming a glorious redhead.

In a book about redheads, there should be at least one section on how to dye one's hair red. As I mentioned above, the majority of redheads today are fake. Unfortunately, there are some horrible dye jobs out there. Most attempts to become a believable redhead fail. I have seen every shade of red, from ultraviolet red to a reddish pink hue most often sported by elderly women. The safest and most natural way to dye hair red is with henna.

What Is Henna?

Henna is an herbal plant extract that has been around for over 9,000 years. It is widely used in North Africa, South Asia, and the Middle East, but it is becoming increasingly popular in the West. Henna leaves will turn almost any surface red. In Islamic cultures, henna is worn on the hands and fingernails and is considered an important source of a woman's beauty. Though it is most often used during festive gatherings like weddings, henna can be worn for any occasion. When applied to hair, henna transforms average-looking locks into superstar reddish manes.

How Does It Work?

Unlike most hair dyes, henna is actually good for your hair. Henna is a natural tannin that stains hair a reddish hue. The resulting color will depend somewhat on your base color. Blonde hair will have a strawberry-blonde tint. Brown hair will turn a chestnut color. Black hair will stay dark, but will have a slight reddish tint. People who have gray hair should be very careful. A full head of gray hair when mixed with henna will become an orangey color reminiscent of Bozo the Clown. In all cases, henna will leave hair silkier and easier to manage.

How Do I Use It?

- Buy henna powder (available in a variety of hues).
- Decide what to mix it with. Anything that is acidic and smells good works

well. Most people use lemon juice, but red wine and other liquids (even water) will also work.

- For added highlights, be creative! Try mixing in other spices/foods. Try tea for golden highlights, chamomile for blonde highlights, or paprika for added redness.
- Let the resulting paste sit overnight.
- The next day, be prepared to get messy. Don't wear nice clothes. Wear plastic gloves so you don't stain your hands.
- Work the paste throughout your hair, from the scalp out to the tips.
- Let it sit for one to two hours.
- Rinse.
- Repeat every month or two.
- Enjoy the new attention you'll receive as a redhead!

Note that henna should not be used on hair that has been straightened, permed, or dyed before. For those people who want to enjoy the benefits of henna without dyeing their hair, henna powder is also available in neutral or colorless formulas.

A chapter on redhead dating might seem a little out of place. How is redhead dating any different from blonde dating or brunette dating? When push comes to shove, it really isn't much different. Redheads enjoy dating as much as everyone else. But our experiences sometimes differ from that of the general population. Here are some special considerations that are unique to redheads:

We Won't Remember You:

A pleasant (and sometimes not) side effect of having red hair is that people will recognize and remember us. We are unique, and whether we like it or not, we stand out. The flip side, though, is that we have a harder time remembering other people. People who recognize us will often approach us and make conversation. Many times we will have no clue who they are. It's not that we are self-absorbed or stuck-up. It's just that our brains have a hard time processing non-redheads. If non-redheads want us to remember them, they should do something to call attention to themselves. Wear funny hats. That usually works.

> According to a Scottish proverb, if you walk between two redheaded girls, you will soon become very rich.

Unwanted Attention:

Because redheads are easily recognizable, we also attract a lot of unwanted attention. This is true in many circumstances, from class, to work, to bars and clubs. This is especially true for redheaded women in the dating scene. One of the biggest complaints I hear from redheaded ladies is that they are easy targets for male sexual advances. Note to guys who like redheaded women: Don't use obnoxious pickup lines.

Supply and Demand:

One of the biggest dating fears that many redheads have is that other people don't want to date them. This fear is made worse by the media. There are few attractive redheaded females on television and in film, and even fewer guys. This is unfortunate. The truth is that many people find redheads very attractive. A recent poll showed that fourteen percent of men prefer women with red hair over all other hair colors. This may sound like a small number, but it is actually disproportionately high. Considering that only four percent of females in the United States are redheads, this means that there are nearly four times as many men who prefer redheads as there are available women. And while I haven't heard about similar polls taken of women, redheaded men should also do just fine. There are more women out there who like redheaded men than you might think. Besides, most women value character as much as or more than physical attributes. Who wants tan, chiseled bodies anyway? Our light-bright skin leaves cool handprints when you press down hard enough.

Redhead Couples:

Nothing brings a smile to my face more than seeing a redheaded couple. Two brunettes walking down the street holding hands just aren't as exciting. For redheads, good things come in pairs. A redheaded significant other is definitely special. Redheads click for any number of reasons. They share common life experiences and share at least a few common interests (an affinity for sunscreen being one). The biggest benefit of dating another redhead? A guarantee that your children will continue the redhead tradition. The biggest drawback of dating another redhead? Everyone will mistake the two of you for brother and sister.

Chapter 10:
Makeup Tips

Redheads are blessed with striking hair and, more often than not, beautiful skin. While they may not particularly appreciate the sun's seeming hatred for them, many redheads grow to love their skin tone. Unfortunately, it can be tricky to find makeup that matches redheads' unique coloring. Don't worry. This chapter will give you plenty of advice to help you look your best every day.

You might be asking yourself why I am qualified to provide sound makeup advice. The answer is, I'm not. I am, after all, a man (albeit a dainty, redheaded one). Despite stealing my sister's fashion magazines whenever possible, I actually know very little about the art of makeup. That's why I enlisted the help of Jayne Cross, a makeup artist in Beverly Hills and a natural redhead herself. As I suspected, Jayne told me that most makeup is not made with redheads in mind. A lot of makeup advice in style magazines is not relevant to redheads. So here is what redheads really need to know:

Traditional Advice:

The traditional advice given to redheads is that they should wear lots of bronzes and coppers. This is generally true. Many redheads do look very good in these colors. But this can also be boring. The truth is, redheads can wear almost any color, provided it is blended properly and it matches their clothes.

Freckles:

Please don't try to hide your freckles. Freckles can be very flattering, even in large quantities. Trying to cover them will only make your skin look fake. If anything, use a very light foundation to even out your skin tone. A light foundation or bronzer can make your skin look flattering while still looking natural. It is much more modern to show off your freckles. Besides, everyone knows that freckles are directly proportional to intelligence.

Moisturizer:

Redheads often have very dry skin, especially in the winter. For this reason, redheads are at risk of developing eczema and psoriasis, skin conditions that are as gross as their names sound. To keep skin healthy, redheads should be sure to use moisturizer on a regular basis. There are countless brands of moisturizer on the market today, and most are non-comedogenic, meaning they won't cause breakouts. Moisturizer should be applied before any makeup is put on, to offset the tendency for makeup to dry out the skin.

Foundation:

Foundation is the cornerstone of many women's makeup routine. Foundation, however, can look very unnatural on some redheads, especially if they have pinkish undertones and try to cover them up with foundation. It's important that redheads use the right foundation; for instance, if their skin tones are warm, they need to use a warm-toned makeup. In my opinion, redheads should avoid foundation if possible. If you must wear it, try to match the foundation and concealer to your skin tone (or go one shade lighter). Apply sparingly! And please do not cover up those freckles!

Eyes and Lips:

Finding good mascara, eye shadow, or lipstick can be particularly difficult for redheads. Traditional black mascara is usually too harsh for redheads. Many redheads who use black mascara end up with raccoon eyes. Luckily, there are alternatives out there. A reddish-brown shade can be more flattering than conventional black shades.

The traditional advice of bronze and copper colors can work very well with eyes and lips. Generally, light earth tones complement light skin tones. Browns and coppers can add a warm glow to your look. Other colors can also work, though. Purples and golds look good on many redheads. But the one piece of advice that makeup artists give to redheads is to throw away that green eye shadow.

The Color Red:

Redheads are often told that they should never ever wear red in clothing or lipstick. This is the one style rule that is given over and over to redheads. It's as if too much red will disturb some balance of cosmic forces. Like most rules, this one is meant to be broken. Some redheads can wear red surprising well. True red lipstick can look striking on redheads, especially with formal wear. Darker-skinned redheads generally look better wearing red than lighter-skinned redheads, but the more sun-fearing redheads can also wear red well.

> Redheads have naturally whiter teeth than people with other hair colors.

Less Is More:

From a guy's perspective, this is the best advice I can give. This suggestion is particularly relevant to redheads, who can easily look like cartoon characters with too much makeup. The best look is the most natural look. Too much eye shadow (or foundation, or mascara) can be very unattractive. Apply makeup in the strongest, most natural light possible to avoid putting on too much.

Experiment:

What works for one redhead will not necessarily work for the next. Contrary to what some people might think, not all redheads look the same! Try as many different looks as possible. Trial and error is the best approach. Borrow your friends' makeup. Get free samples from department stores. Ask the advice of a girl, guy, and maybe your mom.

Other Suggestions:

- Take note of redhead celebrities and models. Julianne Moore, Angie Everhart, and Nicole Kidman are always in the spotlight. Look at their makeup. They employ the best makeup artists to help them with their looks. Copying their looks is not a bad start.
- To spice things up, try to mix and match colors. Try pale-pink eyes with bronze lipstick, or the other way around.
- Be careful not to wear makeup that might clash with your hair. Strong pinks, for example, can look bad on cheeks or lips.

Chapter 11:
Style and Fashion Tips

Picking out clothes that look good on redheads can sometimes be tricky. Personally, I think that redheads look great wearing almost anything. But some clothes are definitely more flattering than others. Unfortunately, most designers do not use pale models with bright red hair as prototypes in designing their new fashion lines. If it were up to me, I would make all runway models redheads. But I'm not Calvin Klein. Until I launch my own clothing company specifically designed for redheads, we redheads will be forced to make do with current fashion trends. In the meantime, here is some general fashion advice to help you look your best.

Traditional Advice:

Traditionally, the only fashion advice given to redheads is that we should wear a lot of earth tones. Tans, browns, soft yellows, and forest greens supposedly harmonize well with our coloring. We are told to stay away from colors like gray, navy, and black because they will make our complexion look sallow. And, again, we are told to never, ever, wear red.

This advice, however, is misleading. Wearing earth tones can get boring, and not all redheads look good in earth tones in the first place. Likewise, grays and blacks do not necessarily make all redheads look sallow. And red can actually look good on redheads. The key is finding colors that work for your particular look.

Skin Tone:

The biggest fashion challenge for most redheads is finding clothes that complement our skin tone. Whether our skin is translucent, freckly, or a teeny bit tan, we have to be careful to wear clothes that work well with our personal coloring.

Most redheads fall into the "delicate" coloring category. The typical "delicate" redhead has a Celtic look with blue or green eyes and some freckles. Julianne Moore has a great delicate look. These redheads have a warm tone about them; they have very light skin with pinkish undertones. Redheads with delicate coloring look best in subtle, toned-down colors. Lilac compliments their complexion well, as do baby blues and pale teals.

Other redheads have darker coloring. These redheads have a cooler tone and are typically Western European with hazel eyes and skin that can actually tan. Angie Everhart is a great example of this coloring. Redheads with cooler tones look best in sharp colors—black, navy, and crisp white are very flattering. These redheads should watch out for duller colors. Soft yellows or orange-reds can be inconsistent with their complexion.

Eyes:

Redheads have notoriously pretty eyes. Girls and guys alike have been known to melt away under the weight of our eyes. Fashion should definitely take advantage of this. Matching a few solid-color shirts to the shade of your eyes is a simple and attractive look.

Glasses:

I have horrible eyesight. I wear contacts most of the time, but I also like the look of glasses. Finding attractive glasses, though, can be difficult for redheads. Dark eyewear can contrast too much with our light skin. Black frames should be avoided. Tortoise-shell or copper frames can be a very flattering alternative. Gold and silver frames can also work well.

Celebrities/Models:

Hollywood is a great source of fashion advice. See what redheaded celebrities and models are wearing. Eric Stoltz always looks fantastic when he appears in public. Nicole Kidman consistently sports breathtaking styles on Oscar night. You can't go wrong by imitating celebrity fashions. Their personal stylists get paid a lot of money to keep them looking good. Though we can't all have personal stylists on our payroll, we can imitate those who do.

Experiment:

Don't be afraid to try something new. If you think that you look good in a particular color, then go ahead and wear it. The most important thing is to feel comfortable in your clothes. Break rules. Wear navy and black if you like. Don't be scared to wear something bold. Redheads do tend to look best in subtle colors, but that should not prevent you from wearing bright colors. Try wearing a fuchsia tie or a pink shirt. Though she is not a redhead, Madonna said it best: Express yourself!

In 1886, a Frenchman named Augustin Galopin wrote in his book *Le parfum de la Femme* that redheaded women have the strongest scent of any women. Supposedly, redheads smell of amber and violets.

Chapter 12:
Red Hair Maintenance

Redheads never have bad hair days, only days when we don't reach our full potential. Given proper care and attention, red hair can look fantastic every day of the week. But seriously beautiful hair requires serious dedication. I think you have it in you, reader. I really do. I sense it from the way you are clutching this book. Luckily, you won't have to make too many sacrifices to achieve your goal of stunningly beautiful hair. If you follow my advice, I promise a glorious red mane second to none.

Hairstyle:

Choosing an attractive hairstyle is crucial to having a good head of red hair. It has always been important. The history of hairstyling is almost as old as humankind itself. Cavemen and cavewomen drew pictures of different hairstyles on the walls of their caves. The Babylonian and Roman aristocracy dyed and curled their hair. And in the twentieth century, various professional hockey players popularized the mullet, the hairstyle of the gods.

Because our hair stands out, we redheads must make sure that our hairstyles are attractive and current. What is considered attractive will obviously change with the times, so we must keep a pulse on trends in hair fashion. Read fashion magazines for new ideas. Your hairstylist will also be able to recommend a good hairstyle, should you choose to try something new. The work, however, does not stop once you decide on a specific style. You now have to maintain it.

Hair Care:

Proper hair care for redheads is not necessarily the same as proper hair care for blondes and brunettes. Our hair is different in more ways than just its color. Recall that red hair is generally thicker and drier than blonde, brown, or black hair.

Our hair care should reflect these differences. The following guidelines will help you maintain your hair's natural beauty:

- Use moisturizing shampoos and conditioners if, like most redheads, your hair is dry.
- Don't wash your hair more often than you need to. Once every three days is enough. Despite what advertising tells you, you don't need to wash your hair every day.
- Mix up your shampoos and conditioners. You might find a new favorite.
- Don't color your hair. Red hair is a lot harder to dye than other colors. Besides, why would you want to?
- Don't smoke or hang around people who do. Smoke will make your hair duller, discolored, and nasty smelling.
- Air-dry whenever you can. If you have a lot of hair, consider getting a special absorbent hair-drying towel.
- Never brush your hair when it is wet.
- Use a wide-toothed comb to untangle your hair.
- If you need to detangle your hair, work tangles out from the ends up.
- Avoid heat and sun if possible — they will dry your hair out.
- Be extra gentle with wet hair. Use a towel to squeeze out water. Rubbing hair dry with a towel can damage your hair and cause split ends.
- Massage your scalp daily with your fingers. This helps promote circulation.
- Be careful while you are washing your hair. Soak in shampoo gently and rinse completely.
- Don't use hot water in the shower. Lukewarm is better for your hair.
- Avoid blow-drying your hair if you can. If not, keep the blow dryer at least one foot from your scalp.
- Contrary to what your mother said, you don't have to brush your hair one hundred strokes per day. Brushing less can improve your hair's health.
- Love your hair and it will love you back.

Hair Loss:

The idea of losing my hair frightens me. A lot. This may strike some readers as vain. Surely my social conscience would have me more worried about the rainforest or saving the whales. Nope. I would gladly sell my soul to prevent hair loss.

There are two types of men in this world: fighters and dealers. Fighters fight hair loss as if their lives depend on it. Dealers deal with it. They shrug it off and accept hair loss as a natural stage in life. I myself am a fighter and proud of it.

Being a redhead is a huge part of who I am. I love my hair and I want to keep it. If this means standing on my head every day for ten minutes to promote circulation, then so be it. I kind of enjoy it. I do have some respect for dealers, though. I wouldn't mind being so carefree about my hair. Most redheads I know, though, are not dealers. Our hair does not necessarily define us, but we are not anxious to get rid of it. Whether you are a fighter or a dealer, there are still some things that you can do to help maintain a full head of hair. The hair-care tips on the previous page should be followed closely. In addition, try to do the following to prevent hair loss and thinning:

- Wash only with a mild shampoo. And when you are shampooing your hair, do not use your fingernails; use your fingers instead.
- Do not color or perm your hair or otherwise allow chemicals near it.
- Do not blow-dry your hair. Pat your hair dry with a towel.
- Do not use a fine-toothed comb. Style with your fingers or a wide-toothed comb.
- Try to eliminate stress from your life. People tend to lose more hair when they are stressed. Try meditation or other relaxation techniques.
- Eat a well-balanced diet with a good amount of protein (hair is mostly protein).
- Exercise! Exercise can promote circulation in your scalp and keep your hair healthy.

Unfortunately, there are no drugs or ointments on the market today that will guarantee you a full head of hair. Better to start now by treating your hair well. That said, it is very hard to fight genetics. I will probably end up bald eventually. But that doesn't mean I can't fight it now.

Chapter 13:
Advice for Little Reds

Growing up with red hair isn't always easy. Sure, your mom loves your hair. Old ladies, it seems, can't get enough of you. But other people can get on your nerves. The teasing and constant attention can be tough to handle at times. You may go through periods in which you hate your hair. You may complain about your freckles. Believe me, though, when I say that this will change. Like most redheads, you will grow to love your hair almost as much as you love ice cream.

Teasing:

Teasing is one of the toughest things that redheads have to cope with as children. It starts as early as kindergarten and can last through high school. The worst of it, though, comes in junior high when hormones run high and insecurities run even higher. Children can be mean, and redheads are easy targets.

Many children are teased for one reason or another. Unfortunately, redheads are probably teased more than most. Conformity and uniformity are stressed by fellow classmates and by the media. Children are criticized for being different, and redheads, as we have learned, are very different.

So what can be done about it? The best advice I can give redheads is to just roll with the punches. When someone asks if he can play "connect the dots" with your freckles or asks if Ronald McDonald is your father, just ignore him. Don't try to fight back, and don't take things too seriously. If anything, a quick wit can be just as powerful as a strong punch. Learn to laugh at yourself. Teasing is not the worst thing in the world. It can help you build up a thick skin and a strong personality. Just know that the same people who are teasing you now are probably going to be the ones kissing up to you when you become successful later.

Unwanted Attention:

Because we stand out, redheads are subject not only to teasing, but also to lots and lots of attention. As children, redheads are accosted by all sorts of people who want to ooh and aah at the color of our hair. This attention can be welcome, but it can also be annoying. And even though you may hate the attention you receive, your mom will probably love it. She will dress you in cute, yet horribly uncomfortable, outfits and parade you around shopping malls for hours at a time. This will continue until you are thirteen years old, at which point you'll refuse to wear silly outfits anymore. The only advice I can give here is to learn to accept the idea of being in the spotlight. This will no doubt continue into adulthood, when random people will continue to stare at and inquire about your hair. Again, this attention can be appreciated (especially if it's coming from cute guys or girls we are interested in), or it can be annoying (if it's from that sketchy guy on the street corner).

Going Incognito:

Another unfortunate side effect of having red hair is that it is impossible to go unrecognized. If you are a child, and especially if you are the class clown, then this can be frustrating. It is nearly impossible to act up in class without getting caught. And don't even think about cutting class. Our light-bright hair seems to be a magnet for teachers' eyes. If you are not in class, then you can be sure that the teacher will know. This conspicuousness will continue into adulthood, so start getting used to it now. Redheads are extremely easy to pick out in a crowd. Like most things, this has its advantages and disadvantages. One advantage is that your friends will always be able to find you at large concerts with no problem. Another advantage is that you will become a favorite target of the Jumbotron operator at baseball stadiums. But this can easily turn into a disadvantage when the whole stadium sees you with ketchup all over your face.

The Sun:

Redheaded children love to be outside as much as other children do. Redheads, and redheaded children especially, need to be extra careful when they are outdoors. Sunscreen, sun-protective clothing, hats, and beach umbrellas should be used whenever possible. Moms can and should remind their children to use all of these precautions.

This can be frustrating or annoying for many children. I have never seen a child voluntarily excuse him or herself from playing so that he or she could put on more sunscreen. Learning good sun care, however, can really pay off later in life. Proper protection from the sun not only prevents painful sunburns, but also drastically reduces the risk of developing skin cancer later in life. More than fifty percent of total lifetime sunlight exposure occurs in childhood. This means that redheaded children need to be extra careful in the sun. So listen to your mom! Slather on that sunscreen!

Be Proud:

Your hair color is incredibly unique. Only a special few are fortunate enough to be born with red hair. Consider yourself lucky. Redheads have an incredible legacy of success and achievement. Many people will go to great lengths and pay a lot of money to imitate your hair color. So enjoy it and flaunt it!

Conclusion:
Are Redheads Predisposed to Greatness?

Our journey into the world of redheads is nearing its end. You, the reader, are now armed with an impressive knowledge of everything red. Whether discussing our humble beginnings as the Pict tribe in what is now Scotland, or spouting off lists of redheaded presidents and world leaders, you are fully equipped to lead any conversation related to redheads.

There is one question, however, that remains unanswered. Redheads have been extremely successful for generation after generation — are redheads predisposed to greatness? If our history is any indication, then the answer is yes. Redheaded superstars like William Shakespeare and Vincent Van Gogh revolutionized literature and the arts. Eric the Red, Christopher Columbus, and William the Conqueror helped draw the boundaries of the Western world. The legacy continues today: we see redheads atop every field from business and politics to music and film.

So how can we explain this? Are redheads a genetically superior breed? Though some redheads might like to think so, this idea would probably not win much scientific support. If anything, our fair skin and susceptibility to skin cancer would make our genes less desirable. A more likely explanation is simple coincidence. We are no more successful than blondes or brunettes, but we are in the spotlight more because of our hair. In other words, people notice so many great redheads because we are redheads — we stand out! When we walk into a room, people usually notice. The same just cannot be said for our less genetically blessed blonde, brunette, and dark-haired friends.

But there might be another explanation. Redheads may indeed be more successful than people with other hair colors. Could it be, then, that nature has blessed us with skills and abilities not given to other people? Perhaps, but we could also be more successful because of our upbringing. Humans are a very social species; our view of the world is shaped to a large extent by how others treat us. Redheads learn from a very early age to roll with the punches. Being teased may fuel our drive to succeed. Our tendency to overachieve could also be a self-fulfilling prophecy. With so many redheads in the spotlight, people have come to expect great things from redheads. Redheads may be pushed more than others to succeed, or maybe we push ourselves more because of our great legacy.

Even our supposed handicaps can be blessings in disguise. Because we burn so easily, many redheads spend a lot of time indoors. While our dark-haired compatriots waste away their days in search of the perfect tan, we redheads can devote our time to more creative and intellectual pursuits. The result? We see a lot of very accomplished redheads with pasty white skin.

There could be any number of possible explanations for redheaded achievement. For whatever reason, we can be sure that redheads will continue the trend of success for centuries to come. So what if we can't tan? I'll take my red hair over the ability to produce adequate amounts of melanin any day. Just pass me my SPF 50 sunscreen.

About the Author

Cort Cass is originally from Pittsburgh, where he is the only redhead in his family. He graduated in June 2003 from Harvard, where he majored in psychology and petitioned (unsuccessfully) for a Redhead Studies program. He recently moved to southern California, and yes, he remembered to bring sunscreen.